ISBN 978-1-5280-5856-8
PIBN 10934654

1 MONTH OF
FREE
READING

at

www.ForgottenBooks.com

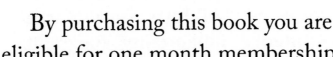

By purchasing this book you are eligible for one month membership to ForgottenBooks.com, giving you unlimited access to our entire collection of over 1,000,000 titles via our web site and mobile apps.

To claim your free month visit:

www.forgottenbooks.com/free934654

English
Français
Deutsche
Italiano
Español
Português

www.forgottenbooks.com

Mythology Photography **Fiction**
Fishing Christianity **Art** Cooking
Essays Buddhism Freemasonry
Medicine **Biology** Music **Ancient**
Egypt Evolution Carpentry Physics
Dance Geology **Mathematics** Fitness
Shakespeare **Folklore** Yoga Marketing
Confidence Immortality Biographies
Poetry **Psychology** Witchcraft
Electronics Chemistry History **Law**
Accounting **Philosophy** Anthropology
Alchemy Drama Quantum Mechanics
Atheism Sexual Health **Ancient History**
Entrepreneurship Languages Sport
Paleontology Needlework Islam
Metaphysics Investment Archaeology
Parenting Statistics Criminology
Motivational

LETTERS

OF THE

HON. C. F. CLEVELAND, and others

Chauncey Fitch

AND

HON. HENRY HUBBARD,

GOVERNORS OF

CONNECTICUT AND NEW HAMPSHIRE,

TO

SAMUEL WARD KING,

THE

CHARTER GOVERNOR OF RHODE ISLAND,

REFUSING TO DELIVER UP

THOMAS WILSON DORR,

The Constitutional Governor of said State,

TO THE USURPING AUTHORITIES THEREOF.

———◆———

ALSO,

THE LETTERS OF THE

HON. MARCUS MORTON,

And others, to the

SUFFRAGE CLAM-BAKE,

AT MEDBURY GROVE, SEEKONK, MASS. AUGUST 30, 1842.

═══════

PRINTED AND PUBLISHED AT THE WAMPANOAG OFFICE,
BY THOMAS ALMY,
FALL RIVER, MASS. SEPT. 1842.

INTRODUCTION.

THE vital importance to the People of these United States, of the questions of Suffrage and Popular Sovereignty, now agitated in the State of Rhode Island, has been the chief reason for the publication of the following letters, in a form suitable for reference and preservation.

For the first time, it is believed, since the establishment of the Declaration of American Independence, has the doctrine been boldly advanced and *forcibly* advocated in this country, that the sovereignty of a State resides in the *Corporators*, and not in the PEOPLE! It will be found from the views maintained by CLEVELAND, HUBBARD and MORTON, that the usurping *Corporators* of Rhode Island find little sympathy for their opinions, or respect for their acts and demands, out of the limits of their own despotic and arbitrary rule. The question—whether the power to change our form of government resides in the governing or the governed?—cannot be too often presented to the American people, as long as it remains a disputed point by any considerable portion of American citizens.—The doctrines of the Declaration of Independence are exactly the reverse of those of the Rhode Island *Corporators*, and are those approved and advocated by the Author of this Introduction.

GOV. KING'S LETTER TO GOV. CLEVELAND.

EXECUTIVE DEPARTMENT. {
Providence, July 30, 1842. }

SIR:—Allow me to introduce to your acquaintance the Hon. Lemuel H. Arnold, one of the Executive Council, who visits you by request, to confer with you relative to the requisition for Thomas W. Dorr, a fugitive from justice, and believed to be concealed in the State of Connecticut, I would commend him to your personal civilities and attention. Col. Clarke, the bearer of my requisition, reported to me, that you declined granting it at that time, but would communicate with me on the subject. That communication I have not had the honor of receiving: and am not advised therefore of the grounds of your refusal, nor do I purpose now to discuss its propriety, but will refer you to Gov. Arnold, the bearer, for the views entertained by this Government. I trust, however, that the events which have transpired since, will obviate any scruples then entertained by you, and will convince you of its propriety, necessity and importance to the tranquility of this State. I will merely remark that this comity between our States is one of the greatest checks against crime, is calculated to produce harmony, and strengthen the respect of the people for the laws and institutions of our country. It is also another evidence of the sagacity and wisdom of the framers of the federal Constitution, which secures to the State this essential right. Not entertaining a doubt of your ready compliance, I would further request that you will afford every aid and facility to accomplish his purpose to Gov. Arnold, who is appointed the Agent of this Government to receive said Dorr, and bring him to this State, and deliver him to the legal authorities thereof, to be dealt with as to law and justice shall appertain.

I am, Sir, with great consideration,
Your Obed't-Serv't,
SAM. W. KING.

To His Excellency,
CHAUNCY F. CLEVELAND, Gov. State of Connecticut.

GOV. CLEVELAND'S REPLY.
STATE OF CONNECTICUT.

EXECUTIVE DEPARTMENT. {
Hampton, Aug. 13, 1842. }

SIR:—I have the honor to acknowledge the receipt of your communication of the 30th ult., by the hand of the Hon. Lemuel H. Arnold, stating that he visits me by request, to confer with me relative to your requisition upon me of the 25th of May last, for Thomas W. Dorr, "a fugitive from justice, and believed to be in the State of Connecticut." Referring me to the report made to you by Col. Clarke, the bearer of that requisition, that I declined complying with it at that time; you advise me that Mr. Arnold is now appointed the agent of the government of Rhode Island to receive Mr. Dorr and convey him to that State, and deliver him to its legal authorities; and you express a confidence that I will aid him in the accomplishment of that object.

When, during the session of our General Assembly, at New Haven, I received your requisition by the hand of Col. Clarke, it was known that Mr. Dorr was not within the jurisdiction of this State, but was known to be in the State of New York. With a knowledge of this fact, I did not suppose, if there was no other difficulty in the way, that you would expect me to do an act so perfectly nugatory, as to issue a warrant, which I well knew could not be executed. As Mr. Dorr remained for a considerable time in New York, and no means were taken through the intervention of the Executive of that State for his arrest, so far as I have any knowledge, I had every reason to suppose that your purpose of seeking to reclaim him as a fugitive from justice was abandoned.—

No case had arisen which either required or authorized my interference; and as you may well suppose, it was with some surprise that in an official proclamation, brought to my notice, from your Excellency, issued some days after and during Mr. Dorr's well known residence in New York, you stated to the American people, that you had demanded Mr. Dorr of me, according to the forms of the Constitution of the United States, and that I had denied your demand. And it was with still greater surprise that in connection with this statement, I noticed your offer of a heavy pecuniary reward, for the delivery of Mr. Dorr within the State of Rhode Island : an offer which, in the connection with the allegation of my refusal to surrender him, could be regarded in no other light than designed to induce an invasion of the territory of Connecticut, or a violation of its fundamental laws, in the unlawful seizure and forcible abduction of an American citizen. I was disposed, however, to find an apology for an act to which the people of Connecticut might well have taken exceptions, in the agitation which I knew prevailed among the people of your State. As it is well known that Mr. Dorr, after the date of your requisition and my interview with Col. Clarke, publicly returned from New York to Rhode Island, and openly remained there for a number of days, furnishing pretty strong evidence certainly, that he was not in any legal sense a fugitive from justice, as you had alleged, I trust your Excellency will see the propriety of my answer to your requisition, communicated to you through Col. Clarke, that nothing had occurred which required an action on my part.

In again calling my attention to the same subject, and requesting a compliance with the same requisition, neither your Excellency, in your written communication, nor Mr. Arnold, as the agent of the government of Rhode Island, in his personal interview, has stated that Mr. Dorr has been found in this State, nor have either of you communicated to me a single fact, tending in the slightest degree to show that he is here. There are no circumstances which have been brought to my knowledge, which led me to suppose that there is the least foundation for the belief stated by you, that he is now within the jurisdiction of Connecticut; and I am aware of no official power vested in me, were I to exert it, to aid your Excellency in the accomplishment of the object which you professedly seek to attain. After a careful perusal of your letter, and free communication with the distinguished gentleman who appeared here in your behalf, I am fully satisfied, as I trust your Excellency will also be, that no case has arisen devolving upon me any duty on this subject.

The case designated by the Constitution of the United States, authorising a requisition and an arrest, is where a person charged with crime in one State " shall flee from justice and be found in another State." But the mere suggestion of a suspicion, or an alleged belief of the concealment of a fugitive, without the slightest evidence to justify it, can impose no obligation for the interposition of the Executive authority of a State. I do not mean that positive proof of the presence of an alleged fugitive should be made in all cases, before any action can be had; but there should be some reasonable evidence, that the party is within the jurisdiction in which the application is made. A public warrant should never be made the mere plaything of suspicion, nor the instrument of private interests. If I am to do any thing in this case, it is through some officer of this State, to arrest Mr. Dorr and deliver him to your agent; but as no intimation is made by you, or your representative who appears here in behalf of the State of Rhode Island, that this man is within the reach of my authority, I am unable to see what public object is expected to be attained, by the present renewal of your application to me.

There is, perhaps, no necessity for my assigning any further reasons, for respectfully declining your application : but the peculiar position in which, as the Executive of this State, I have been placed in respect to this subject, by the official acts of your Excellency, seems to demand of me a more specific expression of my opinions. I say to you, therefore, in all frankness, that if Thomas W. Dorr were now openly in this State, I should feel myself bound to decline a compliance with your demand. I concur with you fully in your views of the importance of that provision of the Constitution of the United States to which you refer, under which I am called to act. It was intended to facilitate the or dinary administration of criminal justice in the several States by reclaiming fugitives from the justice of one State to another; but it was never designed to effect political rights, or attain political objects. To allow the application of this power to the accomplishment of such ends would be subversive of the Constitution itself. An obligation upon the Executive of one State to comply with the demands of the Executive of another State, in all cases and as a matter of course, under the Constitution, I cannot admit. A criminal offender in one State, may be pursued and reclaimed in another; but the forms of criminal proceedings cannot, rightfully, be used to secure personal or political purposes. The Executive of a sovereign State has not only a right, but it is his duty, to look into the circumstances of every case upon which he is called to act. He cannot be made the mere passive instrument in the performance of official acts, nor is it his duty to issue warrants against citizens, without examination, merely because they are demanded by the Executive authority of another State. He must be satisfied, not merely as to the regularity of the proceedings, but as to the nature of the offence of which the alleged fugitive is accused. The term crime within the meaning of the Constitution, does not embrace every act which, through the caprice, or passion, or selfishness, or party spirit of local legislation, may be declared an offence; and the Executive who is called to aid in the execution of the laws of another State, is bound to see that the accusation is embraced in that class of offences to which the Constitution properly applies. If the offence charged be found to be merely an indifferent act, made penal only by local Statutes,—as uttering unacceptable opinions upon religion, or politics, or philosophy, or consenting to be a candidate for a public office,—or if the accusation be found to relate merely to political offences, he is bound to reject an application for an arrest. So he may look at the object for which the prosecution has been instituted; and if he is satisfied that it originated in improper motives, and under cover of legal forms, is designed to attain improper ends, he is under no obligation to aid in the execution of such a process. Where the proceedings are regular upon their face, and the offence charged is one recognized by the Constitution, the requisition of the Executive of one State ought, perhaps, *prima facie*, to be deemed a sufficient ground for the action of the Executive of another State. But if it is made to appear that the prosecution originated in personal malice, or a spirit of revenge, or is the mere attempt to use the forms of criminal proceedings to aid in a private controversy, or to take a citizen into another jurisdiction to subject him to private suits, or attain some political or party object; a requisition for a delivery under such circumstances, ought, in my judgment, to be rejected. If in the height of party conflicts, an arbitrary majority in any State should seek to attain its purposes by oppressive laws,—by establishing arbitrary and anti-republican tribunals,—by abolishing the right of trial by jury, the privilege of the writ of *Habeas Corpus*, a compulsory process for witnesses, and all the safeguards which, in the progress of civilized society, have been thrown around civil liberty, or should abolish the essential attributes of a republican government, by elevating the military above the civil power, and subjecting citizens to unrestrained searches, and seizures, by an armed force, in time of peace and in the absence of any insurrection or rebellion,—the Executive of another State might, rightfully, deny the claims for the surrender of an American citizen to the control of such a power.

With these general principles in view, I am prepared to give the reasons for the opinion which I have already expressed. It is not my purpose to express any opinion as to the various questions which have recently divided the people of Rhode Island: but I cannot resist the conviction that other objects are sought to be attained by the requisition made upon me than the ordinary administration of criminal justice in that State. Under the circumstances which Mr. Dorr and those with him in the late unhappy controversy in Rhode Island have been placed, I cannot regard them as the proper subjects for the executive power of surrender, under the constitution of the United States; nor can I concur in the policy of the oppressive measures sought through your requisition to be procured by the existing authorities of that State. Unfortunately, a great political question, on which the people were divided into two great parties, each claiming for itself to be the lawful government of the State, resulted in a resort to force. In this contest, so far as this forcible issue is concerned, one party has surrendered and the other triumphed; but the great moral and political question involved in the controversy remains unsettled. A proper regard to the prosperity and happiness of the whole people of the State, would seem to dictate to the existing government, measures of conciliation, and a fair submission of the matters in dispute to the peaceable decision of the majority at the ballot box. In their efforts to visit upon their political adversaries the vengeance of the law, they will only widen the breach, already too large, and will hazard their own security and the peace of the Union.

There are certain prominent facts connected with this controversy, known to the American people. It is known and admitted that there has, hitherto, no written Constitution been adopted by the people of Rhode Island as their supreme law, and that the political power of the State is vested in a minority of about one third of the free citizens of the State, over twenty-one years of age, and that a majority of about two thirds of the citizens within the same age, have, by law, been excluded from the privileges of the elective franchise, and from a participation in the affairs of government. It is known and admitted that after various unsuccessful attempts, on the part of large masses of the people, to secure a constitution of government, a Convention of delegates from the various towns in the State assembled in pursuance of resolutions adopted by the people in their primary assemblies, (but not under any authority from the existing government) and agree upon a Constitution or form of government, to be submitted to the people for approval. It is known that this Constitution was submitted to the people, who by the terms of it were legal voters; and it is claimed that it was adopted by a large majority of all the citizens of the State, over twenty-one years of age, and by a number of votes far exceeding any number ever given under the existing government. It is therefore claimed by a large portion of the People of Rhode Island, that this Constitution, thus adopted, became, and is the supreme law of the State; and that the authority of the former officers of government, was thereby superceded. Under this Constitution; and according to its provisions, Thomas W. Dorr was elected Governor of the State by the people—took the oath of office—and attempted to discharge its duties. A legislative Assembly was elected, and met; and under this Constitution organized the government and appointed various public officers. It is also known and admitted, that the authorities of the existing government, and a large and respectable body of citizens denied the validity of this Constitution, and the powers of the officers elected under it. On this question the people of Rhode Island have been divided. One portion have sustained the Constitutional government, and the other portion have sustained the existing one. In the resort by the respective parties to arms, in support of their respective claims, Mr. Dorr and his party have been conquered, and the power of the government now remains with the existing authorities; but the result of this forcible contest, can have no bearing upon the question, whether or not, by law, this Constitution is the Supreme law of Rhode Island, and whether or not Mr. Dorr is the legal Governor. The charge against Mr. Dorr, for which you demand of me his surrender, is the crime of treason against the government of Rhode Island.— Now, it is admitted that all the acts done by him which are claimed to constitute treason were done in the exercise of the duties of his office as Governor, and that if this Constitution was rightfully adopted, he had not only a right, but, it was his indispensable duty to do the very acts in which his alleged treason consists. He did not usurp the office nor its authority—he was elected to it by the people, and it is but reasonable to suppose he entered upon its duties, in the honest belief in his legal right to the office. Whether or not Mr. Dorr has committed an offence, may depend upon the question whether this Constitution is the supreme law of the State or not. This is a mere political question which I shall not undertake to decide. If a large majority of the people of that State, as it is claimed, have, in fact adopted this Constitution, I shall not assert that their act is inoperative ; much less shall I surrender as a traitor, a man whose only offence consists in discharging a duty assigned him by the people, under a Constitution thus adopted. A military force has been successfully employed by the existing authorities, and I am called upon to aid in the delivery of Mr. Dorr to his conquerors. I can take no view of duty which will justify such a course. After a most careful examination of the whole subject, I have determined that the acts of Mr. Dorr, in attempting to execute the duties of his office, and support the Constitution claimed to have been adopted by the people, and the acts of those associated with him in accomplishing the same object, are not of the character which will authorize me upon the requisition of the Governor of Rhode Island, to surrender any of them to the existing authorities of that State.

Soon after the late disturbances at Chepatchet and after the supporters of the Constitution had dispersed, upon a requisition from your Excellency, enclosing to me a copy of a complaint against one Carter, and others, for Treason, and upon information furnished, that he was then in the county of New London, I issued a warrant to the proper officer of that county, for his arrest. This was done without much time for reflection, and amidst an urgency pressed upon me, from respectable citizens of your State ; but on careful revision of the case, I am entirely satisfied that in yielding to that requisition, I did wrong. Upon the principles which I have now stated, Mr. Carter had done no act which would justify a surrender, or demand. Although I committed error, which I sincerely regret, yet it is a matter of consolation to me to know that no injury has been done to this man in consequence of it, as he had voluntarily proposed to return to Rhode Island, before my warrant was issued ; and it therefore had no effect upon the case.

I cannot close this communication, without an allusion to one other circumstance, which if I had any doubts as to the propriety of my course, would remove them. It is a notorious fact that the whole State of Rhode Island was not a long time since, by the existing authorities of the State, placed under martial law, and all persons within its limits subject to the control of a military power. In a time of profound peace, and when no rebellion or insurrection exists to justify it, a military authority is set up which from its very nature, must supercede all civil government, and suspend that invaluable safeguard of civil liberty, the privelege of a writ of Habeas Corpus. It is true that by a recent proclamation from your Excellency, the exercise of this power is temporarily suspended, until the first day of September ; and then, unless some act of the government intervenes, the authority of the military will be resumed. The constitutional right demands, and the duty to surrender fugitives, are designed to aid the civil power, through the intervention of the Courts of Law, but never could be designed to effect the surrender of a citizen to the authority of a military camp.

I have the honor to be, very respectfully,
Your obedient servant,
C. F. CLEVELAND.

His Excellency,
SAMUEL W. KING.

GOV. HUBBARD'S LETTER.

" To Samuel W. King, acting as the Governor of Rhode Island."

As the Governor of the State of New Hampshire, I have received this morn-
ing by Lemuel H. Arnold, a communication under the date of the 15th inst.,
purporting to be a requisition upon me to cause *Thomas W. Dorr*, who is
charged with treason, against the State of Rhode Island, who is represented as
"a fugitive from justice," and who is supposed now to reside within the limits of
New Hampshire, to be delivered to the said Lemuel H. Arnold, appointed by
you as an agent to receive him, that the said Dorr may be "brought into the said
State of Rhode Island and dealt with as to law may appertain."

To this communication I have given all the consideration which the limited
time allowed, would enable me to bestow upon it, and which its importance
would seem to demand. This exciting subject which has for a few months past
greatly disturbed the order and tranquility of the State of Rhode Island, has
not been regarded by *other members of the confederacy* with indifference, or un-
important as connected with the principles of popular liberty and with the inalienable rights of man. The State of New Hampshire, ever sensitive upon these
subjects which effect the independence, freedom and sovereignity of the people,
has through her legislature, at its late session, expressed opinions relating to this
very subject matter. And standing in the relation which I do to the people of
that State, I am happy to add that I fully concur in the sentiments contained in
the report of our legislature touching this subject, a copy of which report I
have placed in the hands of Mr. Arnold, your appointed agent. In the emphat-
ic language of that document " the great question presented is, which is the true
and legitimate government" of Rhode Island, that which derived its existence
from the Charter of Charles the II, or that which emanated from a constitution
recently adopted by the sovereigns of the Commonwealth. " The Rhode Island
controversy has started several questions not new in the days of our forefathers,
but apparently forgotten by us, which can only be solved by the application of
ultimate principles." It is not my purpose to incorporate into this communication, a statement of the events in the order in which they transpired, having a
relation to or connection with that controversy. The public mind cannot be en-
lightened by any restatement of these facts. They have become matters of
public history. And it is well known that the necessary result of certain preliminary proceedings induced the Sovereigns of Rhode Island to appeal to what
they conceived to be the ultimate principles of American freedom, and the
consequences of that appeal was the adoption by the people of a constitution
for the people. And it is also a matter of public history that this whole proceeding on the part of the people, has been denounced by those pretending to
constitute the government of Rhode Island as "revolutionary and illegal," and
the authority organized under the Charter of Charles the second, was induced
to pass an act declaring the "exercise of any of the principal offices under the
People's Constitution an act of treason" and subjecting the offenders to punish-
ment. Under that Constitution made and ratified by the people, a State Government was organized in conformity to its provisions. Those charged with the
public duties were elected and sworn to the faithful performance of their respective trusts. And it is no less a matter of public history that Thomas Wilson Dorr, a citizen of Rhode Island, was agreeably to the requirements of the
People's Constitution, elected to the office of the Chief Executive Magistrate.
That he accepted that office and entered upon the discharge of his responsible
duties, and there is no room to doubt that this is the same Thomas W. Dorr to
whom you have reference in your requisition, and that "the crime of treason"
which you have alleged to have been by him committed against the State of
Rhode Island, in your same communication was deduced from those
public acts, which " in the exercise of his office" to which he had thus been elected by the people of that Commonwealth he had publicly performed.

Having made these preliminary remarks, and having as briefly as possible, for a full understanding of the subject, alluded to the character of the political contest now going on in your State, and to the principles involved in that contest. I will proceed to make such an answer to your request as I shall consider will be justified by the Constitution. I may, however, promise, that I cannot fail to regard the duty devolving on me by your requisition one of the greatest importance, as going to show what are the political rights belonging to man in this country and what political power he can rightfully exercise in his sovereign capacity. In other words, " In whom does the sovereignty reside" in the people or in the Government. In the sovereign or in the agent. My answer to your requisition must conform to the opinions which I entertain upon the question just stated. I could admit that I am precluded from examining the authority from whence a requisition emanates, or the grounds, upon which such requisition is based. I do not believe that the provision of the Constitution of the United States, relating to that subject should be considered as one having an absolute obligation upon the Executive of a State. That he is bound to comply with a requisition at all events. Such a doctrine would destroy the independence of a Chief Magistrate, and make him (perhaps against his own judgment) a mere instrument in the hands of another for the execution of his purposes. This point I shall further consider in the course of the answer.

Believing, then, as I most conscientiously do, that the people are the source of all political power in this republic ; "that they have an indubitable and indefeasible right to reform, alter, or abolish Government as they shall judge most conducive to the public weal ;" that this right may be and should be exercised by them whenever they shall consider its exercise necessary for their protection and safety, in their independent and sovereign capacity uninfluenced by the authority of existing government ; and believing that the people of Rhode Island, in the adoption of a Constitution and in the consequent organization of a State Government, acted in accordance with these great principles, I cannot but regard the Constitution they adopted, and the government they constituted, obligatory upon the people of that State ; and they should be respected by the authorities of the other States accordingly. " If the people of Rhode Island possess any power—if they have any political rights—if they may in fact live under a government of their own choice—then the proper and legitimate government of that State, is," in my judgment, "that emanating from the will of a majority of her citizens." From the earliest history of our republic to the present time, the abstract doctrines for which I contend have been approved by the friends of free government.

In the language of the great charter of American liberty we find these sentiments :—" That all men are created equal ; that they are endowed with certain *inalienable rights* ; that among these are life, liberty, and the pursuit of happiness ; that to secure these rights governments are instituted among men, deriving their just powers from the *consent of the governed ;* that whenever any form of government becomes destructive of these ends it is the right of *the people* to alter or to abolish it, and to institute a new government laying its foundations on such principles and organizing its power in such form, as to them shall seem most likely to effect their safety and happiness." In perfect accordance with this right of freemen, the people of Rhode Island in 1790 adopted a Bill of Rights in which she declares " that all power is vested in and derived from the people," and "the power of government may be re-assumed by the people whenever it shall be necessary to their happiness."

This is the true American doctrine, and is the chief corner stone upon which rests the superstructure of popular liberty and of equal rights. It was the doctrine of those venerated patriots who laid the foundation of this republic. It was the sentiment of Washington himself, who declares in that rich legacy which he bequeathed to freemen, " that the basis of our political system is the right of the people to make and alter their constitutions of government." In the organic law of my own State are incorporated sentiments honorable to her patriotic sires, and to which her sons will cling with unyielding pertinacity. They embrace the great principle of popular sovereignty. It says, " all men are born free and independent ; therefore all government of right originates from the people, is founded in consent, and instituted for the general good."

The same principle is interwoven in all our constitutions. It has become the common sentiment of the freemen of this free country. It was the natural fruit of the revolutionary contest. Speaking of civil government, Roger Williams, the great apostle of liberty, says that " the sovereign and original foundation lies in the people—whom they must needs mean distinct from the government set up, and if so, then a people may erect and establish what form of government seems to them most meet for their civil condition. It is evident that such governments as are by them enacted and established, have no more power and for no longer time than the civil power, or *people* consenting and agreeing betrust them with. This is not only in reason, but in the experience of all commonwealths where the people are not deprived of their natural freedom by tyrants." The Supreme Court of the United States recognizes the same principle, when it says, " A Constitution is the form of a government delineated by the mighty hands of the people, in which certain first principles of fundamental law are established. It is paramount to the power of the Legislature. The Legislatures are creatures of the Constitution. The constitution is the work or will of themselves, in their *original, sovereign, and unlimited capacity. Law is the work of the Legislature in their derivative and subordinate capacity.*

, Such are the authorities which I have considered necessary to present in this answer, going to show what are the political rights and what are the political powers of the people—emphatically the sovereigns of this country. They seem in my mind sufficient to justify the conclusion I have expressed. But it is objected that although the people possess the power " to alter, amend, and institute government," yet they cannot exercise this power without leave asked and obtained from the existing government. I cannot consider this objection well taken. If this be true, the words " original" and "unlimited," as quoted from the Supreme Court, can have no meaning. If the power be " original," it cannot certainly be derived from the existing government. If the power be " unlimited," then the existing Government can have no power to enforce any limitation upon its exercise. It would be a contradiction in terms to say that the people have the right but not to exercise that right but at the pleasure of the Government. This would be to nullify the right itself—to limit its exercise would be to destroy it.—to transform liberty into slavery—to break down the dearest rights of freemen, and place in their stead the debasing doctrine of slavish dependence.

If we cannot abolish tyranny in this land of popular liberty, until the tyrant grants permission, we in effect, give to tyranny an unlimited duration. Such a doctrine is anti-American. Here we hold that Liberty is derived from the grants of no government but is inherent in the People. As a nation we practiced upon this principle when we recognized the independence of the South American Republics and of Texas. Those governments came into existence without leave asked of the existing government. The people of the old American States formed governments for themselves independent of authority. In more modern time the State of Michigan was admitted into the confederacy of States by the independent and sovereign act of her own people without the sanction of her then existing government. And so it was with the people of Rhode Island.— They acted as they had an inherent right to act in their independent and sovereign capacity. They first held a Convention of delegates chosen by the people ; that Convention called another to form a Constitution ; a Constitution was formed and submitted to the people, and was accepted by a majority of her adult population ; when the people passed upon the Constitution they passed all the preliminary steps by which it was brought into existence ; when they adopted the Constitution they adopted the manner, mode, and the whole process used in its establishment. It has thus become obligatory as the organic law of that commonwealth. They not only established their form of government, but they rightfully designated their agents to put that government into operation.

Believing in the correctness of the opinions herein before advanced, notwithstanding the objections made against them, the conclusion of the matter is, that no requisition can rightfully be made on me by any individual acting as Governor of Rhode Island, for the surrender of Thomas Wilson Dorr, who is, in my judgment, its Chief Magistrate *de jure.*

The acts which he did while Governor, were not in violation of any existing law in force, and in no constitutional sense can he be considered as a "*fugitive from justice.*" It has been well said that, "A law which punishes a citizen for an innocent action, or in other words for an act which, when done, was in violation of no existing law, is contrary to the great principles of the social compact and cannot be considered as a rightful exercise of legislative authority." The fact that Governor Dorr was prevented by circumstances beyond his control, from continuing to exercise the functions of his office, cannot change his relation to the people of that State, or make those acts criminal which were innocent and rightful at the time. I cannot, for the reasons assigned, comply with your request.

It may, however, be said that in complying with the second section of the fourth Article of the Constitution of the United States, a Governor of any State on whom a requisition may be made, is only to inquire who is the *acting Governor* of the State making such requisition. This position is unsound. In such a case the most notorious usurper who should happen to get the control for a time of any State, must be recognized by the Governors of other States, and thus they may become his instruments to aid in executing his vengeance against those who may have dared to oppose his usurpation, and who have fled from the State for safety. I am aware that among independent powers a government "*de facto*" is recognized as representing the nation for the time being. This principle rests on the necessity of the case, and on the ground that one nation has no right to decide whether the government of another is lawful or not. But in my opinion a different rule must apply to the States which are part of one confederate republic. The entire theory of our system rests on the principle that all authority is to be rightful and derived from the people—the acknowledged source of all political power. Any pretended Government in any one State not derived from this source is no government at all, and cannot be recognized either by the federal authorities or those of other States. The lawfulness or rightfulness of political power in this country cannot be separated from the existence of such power. If it be not rightful it does not exist. So far then as the Constitution of these United States has required the authorities of one State to do an act in pursuance of a requisition of the authorities of another State, it imposes upon the former the duty of deciding who are the rightful authorities of each State.

I have further objections to a compliance with your request. That provision in the Constitution of the United States in regard to requisitions, does not, in my opinion. embrace *political offences* committed in other States. The language of that part of the second section on the fourth article of the Constitution is, "*a person charged with treason, felony, or other crime.*" Treason here means treason against the United States, which had been defined in the last section of the preceding article—and felony and other crimes means offences known as such at common law and excludes the idea of mere political offences. Would not the consequence of applying this provision to political offences have a direct and inevitable tendency to involve one State in the controversies of another? Should it so happen that a faction in any one State, by fraud or violence gets possession of the Government in palpable violation of the Constitution, and should pass arbitrary laws making it penal and even a capital offence to call in question their authority—and should their opponents flee for refuge to a neighboring State. and should a requisition be made for their surrender, would it be proper to comply with such requisition, and thus aid in carrying into effect the purposes of such a faction? I think not. We were near witnessing such a state of things in Pennsylvania, but a few years since. And it may happen again whenever in this free country an attempt shall be made to set at naught the voice of the people constitutionally expressed. Suppose the majority in a State becomes so exasperated, that in a period of great excitement, they pass severe laws against the opposing party, who to escape persecution flee to other States. Are they to be surrendered upon a requisition, and that upon the Executive of a sovereign State in whose jurisdiction they have taken refuge? Can this be the meaning of the Constitution of this free republic? Can the liberty of the American people rest upon such a principle? I think not. I can give no countenance or support to any such doctrine.

It cannot be that the Supreme Executive of a State, when called upon to exercise his authority to remove a person who is within his jurisdiction, is to disregard the essential principles of civil liberty. That he is not to enquire whether the person to be sent to another jurisdiction is to be punished for actual crime, or merely for his opposition to the will of a dominant and successful party. I think it is not only his right but his duty so to inquire, as it is the first and highest duty of every Chief Magistrate to uphold the principle of liberty, not only in his own jurisdiction, but in other States, so far as he may be called upon to do any official act that may affect them or their people. I cannot, therefore, with that propriety which I hope ever to maintain, and with that regard to the Constitution and the law which I purpose scrupulously to observe, surrender Gov. D. upon your requisition, for the purpose of having him taken to your State for trial upon the charges made against him. I deeply regret the unhappy consequences which have for some time past existed in the State of Rhode Island, and earnestly hope that the time is not far distant when there shall be a restoration of entire tranquility and order among her people.

Dated at Charlestown, this 19th day of August, A. D. 1842.

HENRY HUBBARD,
Governor of the State of New Hampshire.

GOV. MORTON'S LETTER.

TAUNTON, AUGUST 27, 1842.

GENTLEMEN:—In declining to join the 'Friends of Equal Rights' from Rhode Island, in their gathering at Medbury Grove, on Tuesday next, I beg leave to tender to them my hearty thanks for their obliging invitation.

No man has interfered less, in the recent affairs of Rhode Island, than myself. I have had no communication, in relation to the great questions which have agitated and distracted your State, with any of its inhabitants, unless a very little conversation with some of the friends of the old Charter Party be an exception. I have, I trust, been an *impartial* observer of the passing events; but it would be worse than affectation to pretend that I have been an *indifferent* one. Every man alive to the welfare of our common country, must feel a deep interest in the occurrences which have there transpired, and in the principles which they have developed. They have given rise to questions of portentous import to our democratic institutions, and brought to light doctrines which strike at the foundation of all free government.

But what magnifies their importance and renders them of common concernment to the whole country, is the part which a great party, powerful by the wealth and talents of its leading members, now in the possession of the government of the United States, has taken in relation to them.

The people of Rhode Island, acting in their original sovereign capacity, without the aid of governmental regulation, but in a peaceable manner, and with all the formality, which their circumstances would admit, called a convention, founded on an equal representation of their numbers, to form a Constitution for their adoption or rejection. This convention performed the duty required of it, and submitted to the people a frame of government tending to secure equality of representation and universality of suffrage, which was adopted by the votes of a large majority of the adult male population of the State. The validity of this constitution is denied by most of the inhabitants who exercised exclusive rights and privileges under the old Charter. Officers were elected and governments organized under both. It became an interesting question which was the valid instrument, and which the legitimate government. This has assumed a party character, and may be considered indicative of the political principles of the two great parties into which our country is divided. The Whig party justifies the proceedings and defends the principles of the Landholders' Party of Rhode Island. The Whig President doubtless, with the advice of his Whig Cabinet; the acknowledged leader, and supposed dictator of the Whig Party, the Whig Governor of the greatest State in the Union, other Whig Governors and leaders; and all the Whig papers, with a very few exceptions, have taken the side of the old Charter, and those who acted under it; while all the democratic papers, and, as far as I know, all the influential men of that party who have expressed an opinion, have advocated the validity of the new constitution. Indeed, no democrat, in principle, can deny to the people the right to form their own government, or justify that *rotten borough* system of unequal representation which gives to men in one town *ten* or *twenty* times the weight the same number of men in another possess; or defend that restricted system of Suffrage, which excludes one half of the people from its exercise.

The questions, therefore, which are involved in this controversy, though local in their origin, have assumed a general interest, and are brought home to the breast of every citizen for his conscientious decision. Now, without intending to interfere with the transactions of the people of another State, or to give an opinion upon the proceedings of the two contending parties there, any farther than the examination of general principles renders necessary, I feel not only at liberty but called upon, boldly and frankly to discuss those principles.

It is neither my province or my intention to judge of the Constitution of another State. If a majority of the people of Rhode Island are satisfied with their new Constitution, no democrat will deny their right to adopt it, or attempt to infringe the free exercise of that right. But in advocating its legal validity, I do not mean to be understood as approving of all its provisions.

But the enquiry presents itself in the outset—what does this Constitution contain so extremely objectionable and pernicious, or what is there in the old charter so very excellent and desirable, as to justify and require an appeal to arms to annul the one and sustain the other? If the constitution be substantially wise and just, why should not the minority, who had not voted at all, have tacitly acquiesced, and suffered it to go into operation by general consent? If it contained defects, it also contained provisions for future amendments. The only reasons which can be found for resistance to it, must consist in objection to its adoption, or to the principles which it contains. It cannot be presumed that the men in office would expose their State to civil war for the sake of retaining the power.

But what are the great questions involved in this controversy? and what are the vital principles of government which the one party is supposed to maintain and the other deny? They are

1. *The right of the people to govern themselves and to establish their own form of Government.* 2. *Free Suffrage.* 3. *Equality of Representation.*

The friends of the new constitution *necessarily* maintain, and its enemies *necessarily* oppose, these principles. I can see no escape from this conclusion. Let it not be denied that a majority of all the people voted for the constitution. The returns show about *three-fifths*. They have been in the power of the opponents of the new constitution. Doubtless errors were committed, but they have not been pointed out; and it would be unreasonable to suppose that they existed to the extent of the *thousands* which compose the majority. Besides it is a common presumption, that those who omit to vote intend to acquiesce in the decision of those who choose to exercise that right. And this is believed to be the first instance in which a majority of all the qualified voters was required or obtained in favor of any constitution. If a majority of all the people were opposed to the adoption of the new constitution, why did they not turn out and reject it? This would have saved much of ill will, confusion, expense and bloodshed. No: It cannot be so. The circumstances necessarily led to the conclusion, not only that there was a large majority of the people in favor of the constitution, but that its opponents well knew it to be so. Do they contend that the will of the *minority* should prevail over that of the *majority?* Do they maintain that there is a favored class who possess greater political rights and power than their fellow men, and that they cannot be deprived of them without their own consent? *This is the rankest doctrine of* ARISTOCRACY.

Let it not be pretended that the new constitution was not adopted " *according to the forms of law.*" Substance rather than form, is now sought for. The *pettifogger's* plea in abatement, and the *special pleader's* special demurrer, are, in the light of the present day, discountenanced alike by legislative action and judicial decisions. " FORMS OF LAW" !! Constitutional questions are not to be embarrassed by legal quibbles and technical objections. They look through forms to the substance. But what are the forms prescribed to regulate the action of the people in the exercise of their highest sovereign power? Who can establish forms to govern their proceedings?

When the people have adopted constitutions, and in them provided the manner of making future alterations, some persons contend that they and their successors are bound by the regulations which they have made for themselves, and can make amendments in no other manner. Without admitting or stopping to discuss this position, I think that every believer in the doctrine of delegated power must admit, that, in the original formation of a government, the people must, as they proceed, determine their own forms of proceeding. The same rule applies where there is an existing form of government, which contains no provision for amendments. If this be not so, no new government could be formed and no such old one could be amended.

If the community be so large that the people cannot meet and discuss the subject altogether, some persons must *assume* the power to introduce and bring it in some way, before the people for their action. Such was the case in the old thirteen States in the formation of their constitutions; for whether conventions, for the purpose, were proposed by the spontaneous action of the people, or by the recommendation of their Colonial Legislatures, they were alike unauthorized. The several charters never contemplated the establishment of independent governments, and never authorized the charter officers to take any steps towards the formation of democratic constitutions. But however a constitution is proposed to the people it derives all its force from their action upon it. If they reject it, the proposal becomes a nullity. If they adopt it, it becomes the supreme law of the land. The mode of bringing the proposal before the people is not the most material part of the transaction. That which gives them the fullest opportunity for the fair expression of their opinions is doubtless the best. I am not aware that it has ever been objected against the new constitution, that every inhabitant of the State had not an opportunity to vote upon its adoption.

It will not be pretended that the R. I. Charter conferred upon the Legislature the power to propose a Constitution, or to call a Convention for that purpose. It contains not a syllable to that effect. If they did either, they must *assume* the power. As no Constitution could be formed without the exercise of this power, no very strong objection could exist to its assumption by the Legislature; yet as they held unequal and unjust powers, which were the subject of complaint, there could be no peculiar propriety in their doing it rather than a meeting of the people themselves, or their delegates chosen for the purpose. But the assumption that the Legislature alone can initiate proceedings for the formation of a Constitution, and that none can be formed without their consent and preliminary action, seems to me to be founded in the most palpable usurpation. This, instead of keeping pace with the progress of the age, is retrograding some six hundred years into the dark ages—dark indeed for political liberty and the rights of the people—when British Kings undertook to *grant* to their subjects *charters* of their rights and liberties. One man *grant rights* to millions! *Liberties* depending on the *Charter* of a King! Do we derive our rights immediately from our Creator? or do we depend on *rulers,* pretending to be ordained of God, to dole them out to us at their discretion, and according to their good pleasure? Will the American people, or the friends of free government any where, acknowledge the principle that the people can *only* make or amend their Constitutions by the permission of their rulers?

But to recur to the great principles, opposition to which is implied in opposition to the People's Constitution.

I. *The right of the people to govern themselves, and to establish their own forms of Government.* This is declared to be a self-evident proposition, in the Declaration of Independence; is recognized as such in every Constitution which has been formed under it; and has been acknowledged to be an unquestioned and fundamental principle of free government, by the most eminent statesmen, civilians and jurists of our country. This is now, for the first time, brought in qustion, by maintaining, that the people can make, alter, or amend their constitution *only* through the action of the Legislature, and that too whether the Legislature has any Constitutional power to act or not.

II. The doctrine of *Free Suffrage* is a *corollary* or rather branch of the last proposition. The right of self government is inherent in *all* men and not in a *part:* and should be secured to *every one* unless he forfeits it by his own acts. Although this doctrine is not universally admitted, in its fullest extent ; yet few heretofore have carried restrictions upon Suffrage so far as to require *freehold* qualifications. This excludes more than *one half* of the people from any participation in the government under which they live. And they. who are governed by laws in the making of which they have no voice, may be defined to be political slaves.

The Revolutionary axiom that "*Representation and Taxation are inseparable,*" though sound and true in itself, has I fear, had too much consideration given to it.— By placing too great reliance upon it, we magnify the importance of property, at the expense of moral and intellectual worth. No one holds the rights of property more sacred than myself. But I am not willing to put them in the balance, and make them preponderate against man, the noblest creation and the express image of his Almighty maker. The higher and more difficult duty of government is the protection of personal rights and the liberty of thinking, speaking and acting our own thoughts. Of what use is property if our persons are insecure? and why should not those who have personal rights to protect have a voice in the government, whose duty it is to protect them.

But the above axiom is as broad and extends as far as the warmest advocate of universal Suffrage could desire. Who is there exempt from *taxation?* If such a person can be found, it must be one who "neither sweetens his tea nor salts his porridge."

What is there in the possession of land which confers superior intelligence and moral dignity ? What talismanic influence does it possess, to inspire its owner with qualifications, which depart the moment he parts with his land? May not the learned President of Brown University exercise the elective franchise as intelligibly as the most ignorant landholder in the State?

I well know that men who pretend to advocate free and representative governments are in favor of very restricted Suffrage. In France, *only* one person in *two hundred* is entitled to vote, and in parts of England the disproportion is quite, as great. In our own country many desire to restrict rather than extend the elective franchise. But I can see no cause for doing it, and believe they mistake both the genius and the principles of democratic governments. The right of self government belongs to *man* as *man*; and does not depend upon the accidents of birth, or of real or personal estate. And I have seen no reason to believe that power is more safe in the hands of the *rich* than the *poor*, or that the *former* is more honest than the *latter*. I should not, for the highest degree of perfection, look to either.

III. *Equality of Representation* is a fundamental principle of our government, and without it we have no guarantee of its just, equal and beneficient operation. Unequal representation is but one grade better than no representation. Why should men residing in one town have greater weight than the same number of men in another?— Let the advocates of the old charter and of the new convention, which give a disproportion of *ten* or *twenty* to one answer the question.

I have now offered my views of the great principles which seem to be involved in the contest which has been carried on in Rhode Island, and which, theoretically at least seem to have spread over the country, being maintained by those who advocate and impugned by those who oppose the new, constitution, wherever they may be. I have brought to the discussion no personal feelings and I trust no bias or prejudice.— My private feelings are altogether with the officers and members of the Charter party. I have endeavored, as far as practicable, to confine my remarks to the principles discussed. Their application to parties and individuals have been frankly made so far and no farther, than was deemed necessary for their explanation and elucidation. I have not the means nor the inclination to judge of the various acts of the contending parties. Without therefore intending to impeach the motives of any one or wishing to express any mere opinion, I cannot conceal, if I would, that the principles for which I have contended necessarily lead to the conclusion that the new constitution is the supreme law of the State, and of course that the success of the charter government against it, has been the triumph of *unauthorized force* and of *military power* over *political right* and *constitutional laws.*

It is one of the beauties and excellencies of our admirable system of governments, that it provides for the redress of all grievances and the settlement of all controversies without a resort to physical force. And no one has less confidence in the justice of decision by arms or a greater abhorrence of an appeal to them than myself. I yield to no one in respect for the civil authority, or (for reasons which will at once occur) in deference for judicial decisions. I cannot adequately express the depth of my regret and grief at the military movements which have occurred, and the demoralizing and distressing consequences of them. They certainly have added nothing to the happiness of the people or the reputation of the State. They seem to me to have been as needless and uncalled for as they were unwise and injurious.

The unhappy controversy might easily have been settled without bloodshed or resort to arms. There were at least two ways obviously open for a civil decision; and assuming as I do that the great mass of both parties were honest and actuated by good motives, it seems marvellous strange that the one or the other was not resorted to. Either would have produced a decision more satisfactory to honest minds than an appeal to the " *God of battles*."

If either of the members of the United States Senate had resigned his seat; then the election of a successor by each of the legislatures would have brought directly before the Senate the validity of the new constitution. Surely such a step would not have required a very high degree of patriotism in the resigning Senator when thereby he might avert civil war, especially if he, who doubtless would have been re-elected, had confidence in the unimpaired validity of the old charter.

But a better mode of settling the question would have been by an appeal to the highest judicial tribunal of our country. A mutual arrangement might have been made between the contending parties, by which a suit, putting directly in issue the validity of the new constitution, might have been commenced; carried in the most expeditious mode to the Supreme Court of the United States and the earliest possible decision obtained. That the judgment would have been in favor of the new constitution I can entertain no doubt. But whatever it might have been it would have commanded the acquiescence of the whole country, not excepting the people of Rhode Island.

I have learned from published statements, by both sides, that the friends of the new constitution were not only desirous of adopting this course but were willing to suspend all action under the new constitution till a decision could be had. This certainly was meeting their opponents more than half way and seeking an amicable adjustment at the extreme verge of honorable concession. If this proposition was made and rejected, whichever party may be in the right upon the constitutional question, the whole responsibility of the appeal to arms, of the loss of property, of blood and of life, and all the other physical and moral evils resulting from the military movements and government rests upon the leaders of the *Charter party*. I hope their refusal to accede to this most conciliatory, just and reasonable proposal did not arise from an apprehension that the decision would be against them, and a desire by military operation, martial law and other arbitrary and oppressive measures, to overawe the people into the substitution of a less free and democratic constitution for the one heretofore adopted by them.

I must apologize for the length of this communication. It contains the substance of my remarks upon the same subjects made to an assembly of my fellow citizens at Somerset, the only instance in which I have ever fully expressed my opinions. And you would not now have been troubled with it but for the gross falsehoods and misrepresentations which have been circulated in relation to those remarks and especially their reference to certain distinguished individuals in this State, in yours, and at the seat of government.   I am, Gentlemen, with respect,

Your obedient servant,

MARCUS MORTON.

P. W. Ferris, Esq., and others, Committee of Arrangements.

LETTER OF SENATOR BUCHANAN.

"*Washington, August 22, 1842.*

DEAR SIR :—Please to accept my grateful thanks for your kind invitation, in behalf of the committee of which you are the chairman, to unite with 'the democrats and friends of free suffrage' of Rhode Island at their ' Mass Clam Bake' on the 30th inst. I can assure you that it would afford me great pleasure to be with you on that occasion ; but engagements both of public and private character render this impossible.

I most sincerely sympathise with the suffrage party of Rhode Island ; but their sufferings are destined to have a speedy termination. Public opinion, in this country, is more powerful than the sword—more terrible than an army with banners. Millions of brave and free hearts throughout the Union beat responsive with your own—in the cause of your political emancipation. Your gallant little State is now the only spot in our favored country where freeholders and their eldest sons constitute a privileged class, and where the natives of other lands, who have fled from oppresion at home and become American citizens are denied the privilege of voters. This will not—cannot long continue. The march of free principles is onward, and their progress cannot be much longer arrested in the land of Roger Williams. Universal suffrage, and representation according to numbers, are the pillars upon which American freedom must repose. Persevere, then, in your righteous cause ; and by a firm and energetic, but peaceful contest, conquer from your oppressors the rights and liberties of freemen.— Your victory is certain. Yours, very respectfully,

P. W. FERRIS, Chairman. JAMES BUCHANAN.

LETTER OF MR. VAN BUREN.

Kinderhook, Aug. 27, 1842.

SIR :—I have received your letter of the 16th inst. containing an invitation from the Committee of Arrangements of which you are the Chairman, to meet the Democrats and friends of Suffrage in Rhode Island, at a Mass Clam Bake, in Seekonk, Mass., on the 30th inst.

Although I have to regret that it will not be in my power to be present on the occasion I must beg you to convey to the meeting my acknowledgments for their friendly remembrance of me, and to assure them of my most hearty sympathy with them in their efforts to secure for the People of Rhode Island the enjoyment of the rights and privileges to which they are entitled and which are enjoyed by their fellow citizens in the other States of the Union. While I regard the obstructions so long and pertinaciously offered in your State to the establishment of the sacred institution of free and equal suffrage as alike impolitic and unjust, I am happy to believe that they will yet be made to yield to the persevering demands of the masses, and that the principles of equal rights and democratic liberty must ultimately prevail in Rhode Island as elsewhere.

Be pleased to express to those for whom you act, and to accept for yourself, assurances of my respect and regard. Your most obd'nt serv't,

P. W. FERRIS, Esq. Chairman. M. VAN BUREN.

Printed by BoD™in Norderstedt, Germany